A QUICK HISTORY OF POLITICS

A QUICK HISTORY OF POLITICS

FROM PHARAOHS TO FAIR VOTES

Clive Gifford and Steve Gavan

WIDE EYED EDITIONS

CONTENTS

INTRODUCTION

Do you like stories with heroes, villains, rebellion, double-crossing, and, occasionally, death? Great, you've come to the right place!

This book tells the surprising story of **POLITICS** and its many battles of ideas and armies, of thinkers and stinkers, as they struggle for power or the chance to make a difference.

The word "politics" comes from the ancient Greek word "politikos," meaning **"AFFAIRS OF STATE."** A state is an area of land and the people it contains, all under the control of a **GOVERNMENT**. The government makes the laws and rules that people in that state live by.

Governments can be small, large, **KIND**, or *brutal*. So can politicians, the people who engage in politics 24/7.

Politics isn't just for governments and politicians, though. It happens whenever people in **GROUPS** face tough choices and have different opinions on how to get the best outcome. Finding ways to work together, make decisions, and forge agreements can be tough.

Far from being dusty and deadly dull, politics can be exciting, outrageous, crucial, and dangerous. It's often messy, occasionally heroic, and sometimes heartbreaking.

Strap yourself in as this book races you through how politics has developed from dictators to democracy, how individuals have made a difference, and how new nations gained their freedom. Along the way, you'll encounter inspiring campaigners, as well as rotters, plotters, and a real-life rhino that triumphed on election day.

You don't have to be a wannabe president, mayor, or even stand for school council to enjoy the story of politics—just interested in the world around you, how it works, and how it can be changed.

WHO CARES?

You should!

Politics isn't just rich, old men (and a few women) arguing rudely on TV and posing for photos.

From **BLACK LIVES MATTER** and **CLIMATE CHANGE** campaigns to the differing ways countries help their poorest or tackled the **2020 CORONAVIRUS PANDEMIC**, politics affects everyone. Wherever there are decisions to be made and disputes to be settled, politics is usually present.

Your life is ruled by hundreds of laws and regulations—many sensible, some a bit bonkers. Most are created by **LOCAL** and **NATIONAL GOVERNMENTS**. These bodies also fund many things you enjoy (parks, leisure facilities, school) and things you may not enjoy, but are important (policing, waste collection, hospitals... er, school).

You might be passionate about issues such as climate change, discrimination, violence in your neighborhood, poverty or endangered wildlife. If you are, it pays to get engaged with politics because it's the main way improvements can and do come.

Remember how the word **"POLITICS"** came from the ancient Greeks? Well, **"IDIOT"** does too. It comes from the Greek word "Idiṓtēs" meaning a person not interested in politics, people, and the outside world.

DO YOU WANT TO READ THIS COOL BOOK?

NO, THANKS - I'M AN IDIOT.

A QUICK HISTORY OF POLITICS

ELECTED REPRESENTATIVES? PERFECT!

NOW THERE'S ABSOLUTELY NO CHANCE OF THE IDIOTS BEING IN CHARGE.

Now, there are quite a few idiṓtēs in the world and not everyone's interested in or understands all of the issues all of the time. So, in more than half the world's countries today, people called **REPRESENTATIVES** are chosen by the public in elections to look after everyone's interests in politics and government.

But this wasn't the case many centuries ago...

TAKING CHARGE?

Long before parliaments, presidents, and elections, early people wandered the land, hunting and gathering. Sometimes, they had tricky decisions to make.

Over 10,000 years ago, people first began switching from roam to home. They started living in the one place, growing crops and rearing livestock. Life got complicated and decisions multiplied over things like food, water, land, how the community should be organized, and how to protect it from future threats like famine or attack.

How **EARLY COMMUNITIES** made decisions varied. Some groups probably relied on their elders—letting the oldest (and hopefully wisest) people make the decisions.

We call this a **GERONTOCRACY**.

By the way, if you delve deeper into the whole politics shebang, you'll find a lot of words ending in "-cracy" or "-archy." These describe different ways of governing. Here's a couple more that might have been used in the earliest settlements.

MERITOCRACY = rule by people chosen on merit as the most talented or smart.

OLIGARCHY = rule by a small group of people who hog all the power and make decisions that suit them.

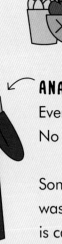

ANARCHY = rule by no one! Everyone has total freedom. No one's in charge.

Sometimes, a single person was in complete charge. This is called **AUTOCRACY** and it became commonplace in early states around the world.

ME, ME, ME

Having a single person in total charge—an **AUTOCRAT**—could be handy in some situations…

We don't know who was the first autocrat, but we do know autocrats sprang up all over the place as chiefs, kings, queens and emperors. In Central America, the Olmecs' sole leader was named Ku, while in Papua New Guinea, they were known as **"BIG MAN."**

MONARCHY (another one of those pesky "-archy" words) is a form of autocracy. Monarchs (that's kings and queens) are usually hereditary—they inherit power, rule for life, and when they die, power is passed on to another family member. Monarchy means leadership based on birth, not necessarily ability.

The "passing on power" bit in monarchies was usually from father to son—girls rarely got the opportunity. **SCANDALOUS!** The Balobedu kingdom (in present-day Zimbabwe) was unusual: it was ruled by a hereditary female monarch called the Modjadji, or Rain Queen.

As the first writers, 5,500 years ago, the Sumerians provide us with the earliest known named monarchs. Mind you, their list of kings is not THAT reliable—King Alulim is said to have ruled for 28,000 years.

BUT YOU DON'T LOOK A DAY OVER 27,999!

One of the first genuine kings was **ME**. No, not me (although King Clive has a nice ring to it), but Me-baragesi who ruled Kish in Mesopotamia. A later king of Kish was actually a queen, Ku-Baba. She's the first female leader we know of for certain. West of Mesopotamia, another monarchy formed. Its kings and queens later became known as pharaohs.

FOR HE'S A JOLLY GOOD PHARAOH

ᴀɴᴄɪᴇɴᴛ ᴇɢʏᴘᴛ was not only a monarchy, it was also a **THEOCRACY**: a state ruled by its religious beliefs, which guided its laws and political decisions.

Egypt's single, all-powerful leader was responsible for keeping the gods (and people) happy and maintaining Ma'at (the religious idea of order and justice) in the country.

Being a **PHARAOH** was every top job rolled into one. You owned all the land, were in charge of the army, made all the laws, and were head of every religious temple. Oh, and you also decided what new cities to build and how fancy your pyramid or other tomb would be when you died. **THAT'S A LOT OF WORK!**

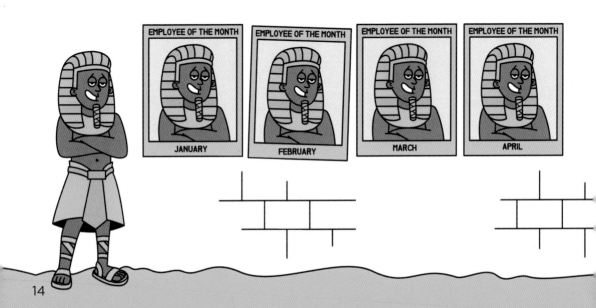

Pharaohs relied on a network of scribes and officials, among the only EGYPTIANS who could read and write. They also depended on their chief advisors called VIZIERS.

Some viziers, including **AMENEMHAT** in 1991 BCE, became pharaohs themselves. Most pharaohs, though, were the son or brother of the previous ruler, although there were also a handful of female pharaohs, such as **HATSHEPSUT**.

Some pharaohs, like **TUTANKHAMUN**, died young. Those who lived long and ruled for 30 years took part in the bizarre Heb-Sed ceremony. To prove they were still fit to govern, the pharaoh had to run round the palace or a special track in just a kilt with an animal's tail attached.

In contrast to the large kingdom of Egypt, ancient Greece was a patchwork of lots of tiny city-states, each called a polis. Something very interesting happened in one of these, around 2,500 years ago.

AWESOME ATHENS

The Greek city-state of Athens had law-makers called **ARCHONS**. One archon, called Solon, introduced the **EKKLESIA** or **ASSEMBLY**—a gathering of all of Athens' citizens to help make decisions. Solon then left Athens for ten years so that no one could tempt him to change his mind.

In 508 BCE, another archon, Cleisthenes, made further law changes and boom! **DEMOCRACY** was GO! Formed from the Greek words "demos" (people) and "krates" (to rule), democracy means a society in which everyone gets a say in how things are governed.

At the time, most Greek cities were ruled by individuals known as tyrants. Athens now had "rule by the many"—everyone who turned up at the Assembly, in fact.

The Assembly met 40 or so times each year on a hill called the **PYNX**, meaning crowded. It was well named, as more than 6,000 men might gather. Everyone present had the right to speak and vote, although men over 50 were often given first dibs.

Athenians were selected at random to form the **COUNCIL**, a group that thought up new laws. The Assembly then argued and voted whether to accept or reject them.

This in-your-face politics is today called "direct" democracy, because everyone involved can vote directly on every issue. In ancient Athens, it could be brutal. In their yearly **OSTRACISM**, people voted against a citizen they disliked. If someone received enough votes, they were exiled... or executed. Harsh!

All this direct governing by lots of people equally may sound amazing, but not everyone agreed...

NOT-SO-AWESOME ATHENS

Some people today think **DEMOCRACY** peaked in ancient **ATHENS**. But it wasn't quite as rosy and perfect as all that. I know we said democracy means rule by all the people, but the Athenians thought differently… In fact, less than one-fifth of all Athenians were allowed **ASSEMBLY TIME**.

More than 80% of adults living in Athens couldn't take part. Those who could had to be citizens. And to be a citizen, both your mom and dad also had to be citizens. If you or a parent were born outside Athens but had lived there all your life, you didn't count.

Nor could you vote if you were slaving away as a slave, a metic (foreign worker), hadn't completed your military training, or were a woman. Yup, democracy in Athens was only for SOME MEN. **DISGRACEFUL!**

Not even all of Athens' male citizens who COULD take part in the Assembly wanted to. Some had to be **ROPED IN**… literally. Slaves holding ropes covered in wet, red paint rounded up stragglers. The red paint was a sign of shame and could be accompanied by a fine.

I'M LITERALLY RED-FACED WITH SHAME.

PEOPLE ARE TOO EASILY SWAYED BY WHATEVER OPINION THEY HEARD LAST.

I COMPLETELY AGREE.

Also unimpressed with democracy were some big thinkers, such as **PLATO** and **ARISTOTLE**. They believed you needed experts to govern and feared democracy led to poor, uneducated people ruling by opinions rather than facts.

Well, that's their opinion.

Democracy continued in Athens until it was conquered by the Macedonians in 322 BCE. It was later taken over by the Romans who, around the time of Cleisthenes, got rid of their own royal rulers.

KINGS AND CONSULS

Athens was unusual. Most states of the time were ruled by a monarch. Athens' fierce rival, the warlike Sparta, doubled up with two kings ruling at the same time.

Rome was also a monarchy until the people got fed up with the antics of their king, **TARQUINIUS SUPERBUS**—crazy name, crazy guy. He murdered nobles, waged constant wars, and demolished ancient religious sites. In 509 BCE, his own head bodyguard, Brutus, led a rebellion against the king who was forced to flee.

NOT SO SUPER NOW, EH SUPERBUS?

Sick of power-mad monarchs, the Romans established a kingless form of government called a **REPUBLIC**. At its head were two **CONSULS** (originally called praetors) who led the army and made laws (sounds like the Romans copied the Spartans a bit).

Unlike kings, though, the consuls were elected and only stayed in power for a year. Once you'd been a consul, you had a 10-year wait to do it all again.

The consuls were elected by the **SENATE**, which was made up of 300 of Rome's wealthiest and most powerful men. They advised the consuls and looked after Rome's money.

In a crisis, power could be handed over to just one man, always a man, and known as a **DICTATOR**. Cincinnatus was a retired ex-consul who was busy farming in 458 BCE when word arrived he'd been made Rome's dictator.

He raced off to Rome, made laws, led the army into battle and victory against the Aequi tribe, enjoyed a victory celebration, and was back at his farm—an ex-dictator—within 15 days. **NICE WORK**.

EMPERORS AND EMPIRES

In 27 BCE, **ROME** ditched its dictators and consuls in favour of an all-powerful **IMPERATOR** or **EMPEROR**. This was really a form of monarchy with one person in charge for life.

Without ways of voting them out, the only way to change Roman emperors was to slay them. Around a fifth of all Roman emperors met an early end, often at the hands of the very bodyguards supposed to protect them.

China was ruled by emperors from 221 BCE, when Qin Shi Huang came to power. He began building the Great Wall to protect the country's borders and reorganised China's money, laws and customs. He was also so petrified of death that he died trying to stop his own. The everlasting life potion he gulped down contained deadly, toxic mercury.

Like EGYPTIAN pharaohs, Chinese emperors were thought of as a link between Earth and the gods. When Japan's first female emperor, Empress Suiko, insisted on being called **"SON OF HEAVEN"** in 607 CE just like the Chinese Emperor, the two countries fell out. They barely talked for the next 200 years—that's a big sulk.

China's neighbor, **KOREA**, was turned from separate warring kingdoms into one empire by the first Koryŏ (Goryeo) emperor, Taejo. Keeping all Koreans under control wasn't always easy, so Taejo went marriage-mad. He wed 29 wives, all from the families of powerful nobles, to keep them on his side.

To govern their empire, Korean emperors copied Chinese emperors' system of highly trained officials called civil servants.

MANAGING ON MERIT

In many empires and kingdoms, it wasn't a case of what you knew, but who you knew. This is known as **NEPOTISM**. Many top jobs were handed out to friends and family, even if they weren't skilled or suited for the job.

HE WASN'T THE MOST EXPERIENCED CANDIDATE, BUT I KNOW HE'LL MAKE AN EXCELLENT LORD HIGH TREASURER!

Chinese emperors realized they couldn't govern their vast empire via jobs for their buddies. Instead, they set up a big **CIVIL SERVICE** to run the empire. It was full of trained officials with tests making sure only the best rose up through the ranks. This is called a **MERITOCRACY**.

Government wannabes studied for years. By 200 CE, one academy was churning out 30,000 civil service students every 12 months—that's more than all the Greeks who could vote in ancient Athens. But only as few as **1 IN 3,000** students passed the fearsome final tests.

Forget your measly school assessments—we're talking **EXTREME** exams.

1. Leave your lucky mascot at home. Candidates turned up at a **GUARDED COMPOUND** with only ink, brushes, food, water, and a pot as a toilet.

2. Candidates were frisked for **CHEAT SHEETS**. Any cheating could be punishable by **DEATH**.

3. The written exams often lasted **THREE DAYS** and **TWO NIGHTS**... straight. If you died mid-exam, your body was wrapped up in a straw mat and thrown over the compound walls.

Those who passed joined the lowest of nine or more ranks of officials. To rise up the ranks took, you guessed it, more studying, cramming, and fiendish exams. Don't knock it: China was governed in this way for over **1,000 YEARS**—about the same length of time as the oldest parliament in the world has been running...

HERE'S THE THING

The break-up of the ROMAN EMPIRE saw Europe split into lots
of small states. In some of these, people made decisions in gatherings
called witans or councils. In Spain, they were called cortes and in
Viking lands, THINGS.

WHAT?

Yup, you read it right. Thing. It meant assembly in
NORSE—the VIKINGS' language.

A big thing, called the ALTHING, was set up outdoors
on Thingvellir (the Assembly Plain) for the whole of
Iceland in 930 CE. Thankfully, it's now held indoors.
Iceland gets chilly.

Those who attended stayed in tent camps called búðir.

From the start, this two-week gathering every June was the social event of the
year. VIKINGS flocked from all over the island to hang out, trade goods,
swap gossip, and par-tay, even if they weren't that into law-making.

But those who were could take part in the ALTHING'S WORK.

26

The main event, politically, was the **Lögrétta**, or law council, where everyone (including important chieftains known as **goðar**) took a fresh look at the old laws and, sometimes, made new ones. A key figure was the **LAGMAN** (law speaker). He had to remember all the laws (no peaking or cheating with notes) and recount a big chunk of them at every Althing.

NOW, WHERE WAS I? ERRR... ALL VIKINGS MUST PAY THEIR RESPECTS TO... PIGEONS ... ERRR...

DO YOU THINK HE'S REMEMBERING THAT ONE CORRECTLY?

WE CAN ALWAYS HEAR YOU, THORD. SIGH...

CAN YOU HEAR ME?

The Althing also acted as Iceland's law court, hearing disputes. One of the first was between the delightfully named **THORD THE BELLOWER** and **TUNGU-ODD**. We're not precisely sure what the dispute was about— possibly, noisy neighbors.

But we are certain that the Althing is thought of as the world's oldest surviving parliament.

TO THE EAST, WESTMINSTER

East of Iceland, other parliaments, albeit with less power, sprang up in Europe. The **ENGLISH PARLIAMENT** grew out of the **CURIA REGIS** (Latin for Royal Council). This meeting—only for mighty barons and nobles—was called by the king, mostly at Westminster in London. Typically, it was to raise more money for wars. In return for the extra loot, his majesty had to listen to a lot of advice…

… but rarely took any of it.

In 1264, a rebel noble, Simon de Montfort, took England's King Henry III prisoner. It was a bit of a cheek, as he'd married King Henry's sister, Eleanor, 26 years earlier.

De Montfort called a parliament, hoping to gain public support. For the first time, it wasn't just big barons who were told to turn up.

Two freemen (ordinary men) from each town were sent, along with two knights from each county. It became known as a **"MODEL PARLIAMENT."**

It didn't do Simon any good— he became a dead de Montfort in battle later in 1265, but when Henry III's son Edward I came to power, he followed the same style of parliament.

By the 1340s, freemen and knights met in one place and nobles and church bishops in another—these became the UK's two **CHAMBERS**, the **HOUSE OF COMMONS** and the **HOUSE OF LORDS**. A **SPEAKER** was chosen from the Commons to speak directly to the king—a risky business. The first Speaker, Sir Peter de la Mare, complained about high taxes and spent most of 1377 in prison, while seven speakers were executed or murdered between 1394 and 1535.

SERFS YOU RIGHT

Whoever owned the land often held the power in medieval Europe. In some places, ALL land belonged to the monarch. They loaned it out to nobles who would swear an **OATH OF LOYALTY** or allegiance to the king along with promises to provide armies and money.

In some places, the **LAND-FOR-LOYALTY** deal had several more tiers, with **BARONS** and **LORDS** loaning land out to **KNIGHTS**, and knights letting small plots of land to ordinary working people—**PEASANTS** or **SERFS**. This system was later called **FEUDALISM**.

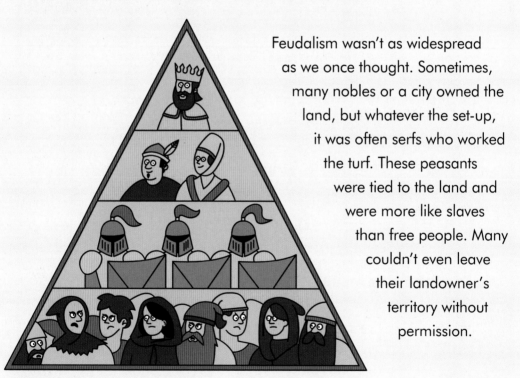

Feudalism wasn't as widespread as we once thought. Sometimes, many nobles or a city owned the land, but whatever the set-up, it was often serfs who worked the turf. These peasants were tied to the land and were more like slaves than free people. Many couldn't even leave their landowner's territory without permission.

SERFS had few rights and definitely no vote. They had to look after the landowner's fields as well as their own, and hand over a share of their own crops for the opportunity. Harsh! If your parents were serfs, then you were born one. It was a tough gig, but most serfs knew their place…

Serf Required

Contract: for life

Duties: back breaking labor

Wages: what you're given

Opportunities for promotion: none

Benefits: a meager existence

Holiday: death

DID YOU KNOW? THE WORD "ROBOT" COMES FROM THE CZECH "ROBOTA," MEANING SERF LABOR.

… Well, most of the time. In the 12th and 13th centuries, serfs rebelled in parts of northern Europe. Many also escaped the countryside for freedom in growing towns and cities. Serfdom started dying out in western Europe, but continued in eastern Europe into the 19th century.

SHOCKING!

But not as shocking as the tactics of one Italian diplomat…

NAUGHTY NICCOLÒ

Medieval Italy was packed with
bickering little city-states. One, the **Florentine
Republic**, employed a diplomat who wrote poetry
and comedies in his spare time, but is now
thought of more like a cunning supervillain.

Niccolò Machiavelli's day job meant he plotted
and planned for a living. One of his strangest
schemes was hatched with famed brain Leonardo da Vinci.
The pair planned to **STEAL A RIVER**, the Arno, by diverting it away from
Pisa, a rival city. They failed.

What sealed Nicco's **RUTHLESS REPUTATION** was his book on how to seize
power and hold onto it. *The Prince* was published in 1532, five years after
his death. It was a warts n' all guide to government of the time.

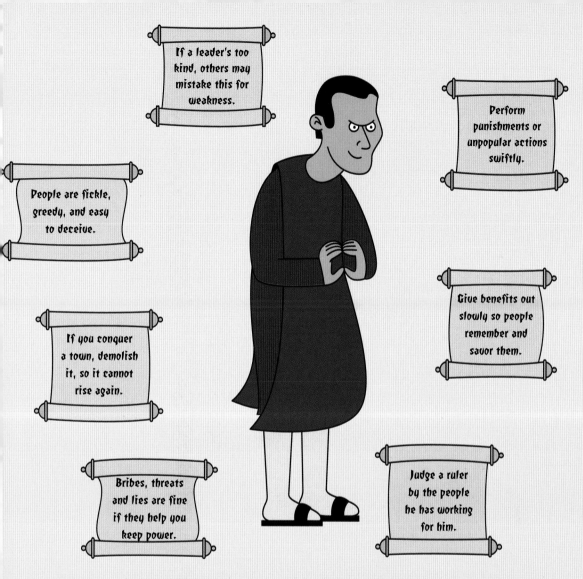

If a leader's too kind, others may mistake this for weakness.

Perform punishments or unpopular actions swiftly.

People are fickle, greedy, and easy to deceive.

If you conquer a town, demolish it, so it cannot rise again.

Give benefits out slowly so people remember and savor them.

Bribes, threats and lies are fine if they help you keep power.

Judge a ruler by the people he has working for him.

Machiavelli's practical tips on power shocked, but proved influential. *The Prince* was one of the few things the Catholic and Protestant churches agreed on—both banned the book. Will Shakespeare even began calling the villains in his plays **"Machiavels."**

Many politicians and rulers, however, would tut-tut about the book in public and then follow its suggestions in private. Some continue to do so to this day.

Throughout history, this has had mixed results...

PARLIAMENT 1, KING 0

Some power-hungry types in the 17th century obviously didn't get Machiavelli's memos. They found power hard to hold onto.

The century started **EXPLOSIVELY** with a 1605 plot by **GUY FAWKES** and others to use gunpowder to blow up the whole Houses of Parliament…

The century stayed lively as assemblies of law-makers clashed with absolute monarchs who thought they were above the law. European kings claimed a "divine right to rule"—the idea that their power came from God.

One solution was to close the assembly down, which was the fate of France's Estates-General in 1614—for over 170 years. Ouch! Across the Channel in England, the thin-skinned King Charles I shut Parliament down in 1629 after he broke laws and faced criticism.

When Parliament reopened in 1640, it refused King Charles' request for more money and passed laws to limit his power. This was too much for Charlie, who stormed the House of Commons in 1642 to arrest five members of parliament (MPs) himself.

COME ON! IT TAKES MONEY TO MAINTAIN THESE LUSCIOUS LOCKS!

THE ENGLISH CIVIL WAR began pretty much straight after and lasted until 1651. It pitted **CAVALIERS** (who supported the king) against **ROUNDHEADS** (who supported Parliament). Parliament won and the king lost his head (literally).

WAIT, I'M A CAVALIER!

BUT YOU LOOK LIKE A ROUNDHEAD.

The monarchy returned in 1660 with King Charles II, but it no longer had absolute power. Parliament had bared its teeth. Grrrr. It continued to grow as the king or queen became less important and more of a figurehead. This suited one political thinker down to the ground.

LOCKE'S THE KEY

JOHN LOCKE'S dad fought against King Charles I during the English Civil War so perhaps it's no surprise that his son was not crazy about kings and queens, especially those who claimed an absolute right to rule.

> MY DAD COULD BEAT UP YOUR DAD!

> AND DID!

A-List philosopher Locke believed that everyone was created equal, so no one should be placed high above all the others. He also thought that nature gave people **"NATURAL RIGHTS,"** such as the rights to life, freedom, and property.

According to Locke, people can agree to give up some of their natural rights to a government, providing it protects the rest of their rights. He reckoned any government that failed to do so should be booted out. What a rebel!

JOHN LOCKE:
A REAL
POLITICAL REBEL

Locke's idea of power coming from the people, not God, was pretty radical at a time when absolute monarchs still ruled most of Europe. But Locke stopped short of recommending direct democracy (see page 17) or elections for all. He believed that a mix of elected representatives and aristocracy should govern and only men who owned property should vote in elections. **BOO!**

Across the English Channel in the 1740s, French philosopher **CHARLES MONTESQUIEU** liked much of Locke's thinking, but feared that even without absolute monarchs, all the power could still end up in the hands of one person or a small group of power-hungry elties. So, he suggested splitting up the main parts of running a country (making laws, judging laws, and carrying out laws) into **THREE SEPARATE BRANCHES** so that no one became too powerful.

YOUR TRIPLE CONE, BARON.

AHH PERFECTLY BALANCED. THREE IS MY FAVOURITE NUMBER!

This separation of powers would be adopted by a number of new nations, but only after they became independent and had wrestled free of the control of other countries.

AGE OF EMPIRES

From the 17th century onward, a handful of European countries invaded and took over much of the world. Portugal, France, Spain, and Britain, among others, sent ships and soldiers to explore and then conquer large parts of other continents.

There, they violently seized land, power, and valuable resources such as foods, silver, and spices. They also captured thousands of men and women as slaves.

Each new territory claimed for a country was called a **COLONY**. Sometimes, colonies changed hands as the European powers fought each other.

EMPIRES grew and grew. At its peak, Spain's equaled one-eighth of all the world's land. That's huge, yet not the biggest. Despite losing colonies when the US became independent, Britain's empire grew to contain a fifth of the world's land and people by the early 19th century.

A sudden **"SCRAMBLE FOR AFRICA"** in the 19th century saw almost the whole continent divided up by a handful of European countries. New, straight line borders were drawn, cutting through traditional boundaries and splitting up the people who lived there.

How were these colonies governed? Often brutally, with the local people treated extremely harshly. Most of the French colonies were ruled directly by the government in France. Other colonies were ruled indirectly, where a colonial power hand-picked local people to do what they told them to.

Most native people lost land and wealth and were expected to work and pay taxes, yet with no representation in politics. Overall, vast amounts of wealth and resources were **STOLEN** from the colonized countries by the **EUROPEAN INVADERS**. Some colonies, though, began fighting back...

I WANT TO BREAK FREE

On July 2nd, 1776, **13 COLONIES** in **NORTH AMERICA** voted to break away from British rule. Two days later, once the wording was agreed, they went public. Now, saying you're independent and becoming independent are two different things.

It can take a fair old time to actually get free, as the US found over seven years of battling Britain.

But in 1783, the **TREATY OF PARIS** was signed, recognizing the United States of America as a brand-new nation. Hurrah! All the USA now had to do was choose its own political system.

The **FOUNDERS** of the US were very keen on democracy but knew they couldn't operate direct democracy like in ancient Athens (see pages 16–19). For starters, they had far too many voters to cram into one town.

These voters also lived long distances from each other. They couldn't all just nip into the same place every time a vote was needed. So, **REPRESENTATIVE DEMOCRACY** was plumped for. This is where a group of people in an area elect a person to represent them and their interests.

These and many other points were written up in 1787 to form the US **CONSTITUTION**—a set of rules organizing how a nation should be run. It was just four pages and 4,500 words long (India's 1949 constitution stretched to 146,000 words). It's since been added to by 27 changes called **AMENDMENTS** and sets out how the different branches of government work.

YOU'LL HAVE TO WRITE SMALLER THAN THAT. WE'LL BE AMENDING THIS THING LIKE CRAZY!

we the people...

AMERICA DECIDES

Many early Americans wanted to avoid an all-powerful government—they'd had enough of that when ruled by the Brits! So, recalling Montesquieu's ideas (see page 37), they decided to split the government into **THREE SEPARATE BRANCHES**: executive, legislative, and judicial.

The **EXECUTIVE**, headed by a **PRESIDENT**, carries out laws and can suggest new ones. The Prez makes agreements with other countries, picks ministers, appoints judges to the Supreme Court (the top court), and is the military's commander-in-chief. Atten-shun!

The **LEGISLATURE**, called the **US CONGRESS**, debates and passes laws. It's split into two houses, the **HOUSE OF REPRESENTATIVES** (now with 435 members) and the **SENATE** (with 100 senators, two from each state). All its members are voted for in elections.

The **JUDGES** that make up the **JUDICIARY** check the other two branches aren't breaking the rules. They can decide that an action taken by the president or a law passed by Congress goes against the constitution.

AS PRESIDENT, I DECLARE THAT THE JUDICIARY SHOULD HAVE TO WEAR THESE FUN WIGS, LIKE THE BRITS.

MOTION DECLINED!

Each branch can put the brakes on another branch. Congress can pass a law, but the president can veto (reject) it, while the president's appointments have to be approved by the Senate. These **CHECKS** and **BALANCES** were designed to stop one branch hogging all the power. But they can lead to new laws and actions getting tangled up in government and delayed. Some never get free.

POOR GUY—HE'S BEEN TRYING TO PASS THAT LAW SINCE 1793.

US presidents are elected every four years, with the first being George Washington. As old Hippo Teeth* was elected in 1789, things were getting really revolting in France...

*Washington wore dentures made of hippopotamus ivory, human teeth, and metals.

THE PEASANTS ARE REVOLTING!

Back across the Atlantic, by the 1780s, many French people were poor, hungry, powerless, and heavily taxed. Those in power—the nobles, church, and King Louis XVI—were mega-rich. The king and his wife, Marie Antoinette, spent **BIG**, but in 1789 called representatives of the French people to the Estates-General assembly to ask for more money. Oh, the cheek of it.

PLEASE HELP, I'M DOWN TO MY LAST 40 FUR CAPES AND MY WIFE HAD TO CUT HER SILK GLOVE ORDER TO JUST SIX PAIRS A DAY.

Instead of cash, all the king got was earache from *complaints*. The people's representatives continued to meet and called themselves the **NATIONAL ASSEMBLY**. They vowed (at an indoor tennis court) to create a new constitution for France with lots of freedoms and rights for ordinary people.

I THOUGHT IT WAS MIXED DOUBLES?

When the king plotted to remove the assembly, mobs stormed parts of Paris. *Revolution, riots, terror,* and *turmoil* swept France for a decade. The National Assembly declared every citizen should be equal and overthrew the monarchy. Thousands were *killed* in battles or *executed*, including the king and his wife, using a razor-sharp guillotine.

French soldier **NAPOLEON** seized power in 1799 and five years later crowned himself emperor. The **FRENCH REVOLUTION** had ended up ousting one absolute ruler (Yay!) and replacing him with another (Boo!). But it wasn't a total failure.

Its impact changed France forever, and its ideas—such as freedoms for ordinary people and representative democracy—influenced politics and inspired revolutions elsewhere. It also led to the use of "left" and "right" to describe political viewpoints and parties.

LEFT OR RIGHT

When **FRANCE'S NATIONAL ASSEMBLY** first met, those who wanted change sat on the **LEFT** of the room. The king's supporters (some of whom lost their heads later) sat on the **RIGHT**. Over time, right and left became a simple, broad way to describe **POLITICAL VIEWPOINTS**.

Many to the **RIGHT** are conservatives who believe in tradition and largely keeping things the way they are or were. They may feel it's up to individuals to improve their own lives and that everyone has a duty to help their country. Sometimes (but not always), conservatives prefer government to be small and not to interfere much in people's lives or tie up businesses with laws and things like health and safety regulations (nicknamed red tape).

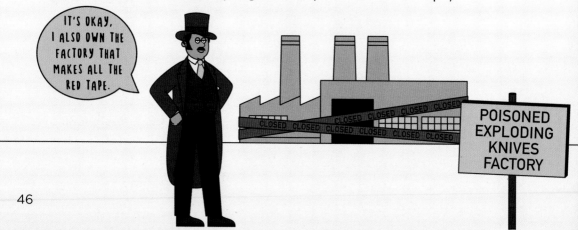

IT'S OKAY, I ALSO OWN THE FACTORY THAT MAKES ALL THE RED TAPE.

POISONED EXPLODING KNIVES FACTORY

To the **LEFT** are people who believe things need changing, society should be more equal, and the government has a duty to help. Many on the left believe government should take action to protect people's rights and freedoms. Some (but not all) on the left believe that government should raise higher taxes and redistribute some wealth from rich to poor.

Now, people are complex and, frankly, baffling. Some people lean to the left on some issues and to the right on others. Others hold extreme views which put them to the far left, like communism, or far right, like fascism. Lots hold views that fall between left and right, placing them in what is called the **CENTER**.

Despite all these different viewpoints, people found ways of gathering together in groups of similar-minded people. Time for a party…

PARTY TIME!

People band together in a **POLITICAL PARTY** in the hope of winning elections and gaining political power. Parties are groups of people who share many of the same political views. Not all, though, which explains those heated party arguments you sometimes hear about in the news.

A faction is smaller than a party—this is a group of politicians who work together, but usually break up when they don't gain power. The first political parties (the Whigs and Tory Party in England) grew out of factions like the Rockingham Whigs in the 17th century.

PARTIES change over time, splitting up or merging with others. Today, most countries have a handful of major political parties and dozens of smaller ones, including the Donald Duck Party in Sweden, the Stay Awake Party in India, and the Rubbish Party in Scotland (anti-littering) which won a council seat in 2017.

DON'T WASTE YOUR VOTE: VOTE RUBBISH!

Parties provide voters with choices come election time. When they don't gain power, political parties can act as opposition, questioning and criticizing governments and keeping them on their toes. Anyone can join a party, many of which have special sections for younger people.

Not all countries leave voters spoiled for choice. Some countries, such as Jamaica and Malta, have **JUST TWO PARTIES** that dominate their politics. One of the biggest two-party systems is the US.

DEMOCRATS and **REPUBLICANS** form the two major US parties today. But back at the end of the 18th century, the first parties in the US were the Federalists and the Democratic-Republicans. They fought over the amounts of power given to the country's states and its national government.

PARTY ANIMALS: THE DEMOCRATS USE A DONKEY AS THEIR SYMBOL, WHILE THE REPUBLICANS HAVE AN ELEPHANT.

FED UP

While many countries had a single, central government in the 1700s, the writers of the **US CONSTITUTION** felt it was good to share and that **FEDERALISM** was the way to go.

In federal countries, power and the authority to make laws is shared between different **TIERS OF GOVERNMENT**. This means national governments are in charge of some areas of law, and regional governments in charge of others.

The US gave its federal (national) government the powers, among others, to make money (ker-ching!), fight piracy (aaarghhh!), raise armies, and control trade between states and with other countries.

The states were given all the other powers not granted to the federal government. This included powers in education, health, and to hold elections. Sounds smooth, but as the US and its government have grown, there've been plenty of clashes between the states and federal government.

Throughout the history of the USA, hundreds of legal battles have been fought over who has the right to set each law.

Despite all this wrangling, many other countries also fancied getting the federal feeling, including **MEXICO** in 1828 and **AUSTRALIA** in 1901. **GERMANY,** too, is federal, split up into 16 states called Länder each with their own constitution, government and law-making powers. Strange laws in Germany include being allowed to drive naked in one's car, but not being allowed to practice musical instruments after 8.00 p.m.!

INDIA, CANADA, and **BRAZIL** are also federal nations, with their land divided up into separate states, provinces, or territories. Further divvying up is needed to create the separate voting areas or districts that choose politicians during election time.

DIVVYING IT UP

Fiji, Serbia, Israel, and a few other countries don't spl-*it* come national election time. They treat the whole country as one, **SINGLE VOTING DISTRICT**.

Elsewhere, most nations delimit, meaning they divvy themselves up into smaller areas known as **ELECTORAL DISTRICTS** or **CONSTITUENCIES**. Iceland has a slim 6 constituencies, while the UK has 650. Greedy, eh?

A special electoral organization or part of the government in some nations decides how many representatives get elected from each area—known as apportionment.

People vote for candidates in their area and the winners represent that area in politics. **REPRESENTATIVES** can speed up and slim down politics. Sounds cool, but these systems aren't perfect.

In the past, there was no computing or accurate, up-to-date figures about who lived where. Voting areas were sometimes based on traditional divisions of land from centuries earlier.

In England until 1832 (when reforms were made), some constituencies had next-to-no voters. Old Sarum, for instance, elected two MPs yet contained just 11 voters. MPs were also elected to represent the constituency of Dunwich even though most of it was underwater, reclaimed by the sea!

AH, THE MEMBER FOR DUNWICH, I PRESUME?

In parts of 19th-century **HUNGARY**, just 150 votes were enough to win in some places, while you might need over 9,000 votes in others. Some local and state elections varied even more. In **CALIFORNIA** in the early 1960s, one voting district contained 14,000 voters, another over 6 million—yet both elected one state senator. Not fair!

To make voting even more unfair, some unscrupulous people in power pulled out a pen and redrew the shapes of voting areas on maps...

GERRYMANDERING

In some countries, voting areas can be changed every now and then by whoever was in power. Some ruling politicians choose to **REDRAW** voting areas' boundaries to favor their side.

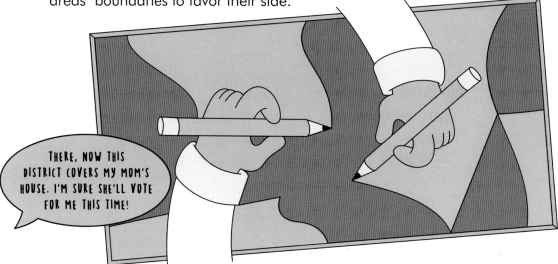

THERE, NOW THIS DISTRICT COVERS MY MOM'S HOUSE. I'M SURE SHE'LL VOTE FOR ME THIS TIME!

They might do this by **PACKING** all or most of their opponents' voters into one voting area. Sure, they'd lose that one area, but this slashed their opponents' chances in all the other areas.

Or they might get **CRACK ING**. This is splitting opponents' votes up across many voting areas to weaken them everywhere.

At an 1812 election, a redrawn voting district in the US state of Massachusetts was so oddly shaped it looked like a cross between a dragon and a **SALAMANDER** lizard. A political cartoon publicized the redrawing, which had been ordered by the state's governor, **ELBRIDGE GERRY**. The word **GERRYMANDERING** was born.

EVEN WITH FEWER RED VOTES THAN BLUE, RED WINS 3 DISTRICTS TO 2 THANKS TO SOME CRAFTY PACKING AND CRACKING.

It didn't do Gerry much harm; he won his election and the year after became vice president. **GERRYMANDERING** continued in many nations. In the 1962 Bahamas national election, gerrymandering resulted in the winning United Bahamian Party gaining more than twice as many seats as their main opponents even though they gained far fewer votes.

WELL, I THINK I'M BEAUTIFUL JUST THE WAY GERRY DREW ME.

THE ABOMINABLE GERRYMANDER

Sick of gerrymandering in her home state of Michigan, 26-year-old Katie Fahey posted a Facebook message in 2016 asking others to help her stop it. Two years later, her idea gained enough votes at an election. So, the next time the state's districts were redrawn in 2021, it was not by politicians, but by a **COMMITTEE** of 13 ordinary people. Way to go!

But ordinary people banding together to get their voices heard is nothing new...

REBEL, REBEL

In the 19th century, as the Industrial Revolution took hold in many countries, millions had moved to cramped, crowded cities and towns. Work, pay, and living conditions were often dreadful.

Many people felt they were being exploited (taken unfair advantage of) and the revolutions in America and France had shown what was possible if people rebelled.

Waves of **DEMONSTRATIONS** and **REBELLIONS** kicked off throughout Europe, particularly in 1820, 1830, and 1848–49. These demanded independence, a change of ruler or laws, or the right to vote (still only reserved for wealthy, land-owning men).

Many governments used force to stop protests. At the Peterloo Massacre in 1819, for instance, cavalry charged into a peaceful crowd of 50,000 demonstrators in Manchester, England, injuring or killing over 600 people.

Other countries, though, made reforms to try to keep people happy. Greece, France, and Denmark, for instance, all passed laws allowing more (but still, all men) the right to vote.

Most of the revolutions and rebellions failed, but some removed rulers, such as the very last king of France, Louis-Philippe, in 1848. (Yes, I know France got rid of kings during the French Revolution, but they'd crept back, in 1814.) Rebellions also helped small states eventually unite into the large countries of Italy and Germany.

One pamphlet, published in 1848, predicted more revolutions to come. It was called The **COMMUNIST MANIFESTO.**

MARX MY WORDS

The **COMMUNIST MANIFESTO** of 1848 was the work of two German philosophers, **KARL MARX** and **FRIEDRICH ENGELS**. Next to no one read the 23-page pamphlet at the time. Millions did later, along with Marx's much bigger book, **DAS KAPITAL***, all 2000+ pages of it.

WE BELIEVE IN TWO THINGS: BIG BOOKS...

... AND BIG BEARDS.

Marx found himself hounded out of country after country for his views. He was expelled from Germany as well as Belgium and France, and settled in London, where he lived in poverty. It's said that some days, he couldn't leave his house because his wife, Jenny, had pawned his only pants to get money for food.

Marx saw politics as a **STRUGGLE** between two different classes of people—the many, many **WORKERS** (the proletariat) and the far fewer **WEALTHY AND POWERFUL** (the bourgeoisie).

KARL, YOUR PRIVATE PROPERTY IS SHOWING.

He thought that eventually **REVOLUTION** would lead to the rich being toppled by the poor on the way to a fairer society where everyone had an equal share.

Marx believed that there should be **NO PRIVATE PROPERTY**. Instead, the state, not individuals or companies, should own the **"MEANS OF PRODUCTION."** These are all the things that make goods or money, including factories, farms, shops, and industries. Marx said that the profits from these should go back into the country so they could be shared out equally.

Marx's ideas (known together as Marxism) fueled many **SOCIALIST** and **COMMUNIST** parties, some of which seized power in their countries (see pages 70–71). Marxism also inspired many individuals who felt exploited to make their voice heard at the polling booth.

*Kapital is German for "capital," meaning money and financial assets.

THE ART OF PERSUASION

In the 18th and early 19th centuries, it was all out in the **OPEN**, elections wise. People voted in public, sometimes via a show of hands or shouting out their choice from a platform. Voters often left the platform to boos or abuse from supporters of other politicians.

UH... I VOTE FOR WHOEVER THIS GUY DIDN'T.

In some countries, your name and voting choice was published in newspapers or poll books. It could make for uncomfortable reading.

Voting in this way was called an **OPEN BALLOT** and was easy to influence. How? By either being really nice or really nasty to voters.

Some candidates "treated" voters by giving them free meals, gifts, or cold, hard cash. At an 1868 election in Beverley, England, the Conservatives gave money to over a third of all voters. The Liberals did the same in the election three years earlier. They slid £1–£4 (a lot of money at the time) through a small hole in the local library's front door.

A **nastier** alternative was to place feared, local strongmen or bludgeon gangs armed with weapons close to where people voted to intimidate, influence, and sometimes beat voters.

HE MAKES A PERSUASIVE ARGUMENT.

VOTE

In 1856, Tasmania, Australia, became the first place to use **SECRET BALLOTS**. A voter gave their name to officials and was handed a ballot paper with the candidates' names. They entered a private booth, marked their choice, folded the paper, and slipped it into a box. Simples.

SECRET BALLOT THIS WAY

A secret ballot means no one else knows who you voted for, making it harder for treatings or beatings to influence elections unfairly. This system was adopted elsewhere in Australia and in other countries from the 1870s onward.

MOST VOTES WINS

Whether voting in secret or out in the open, most 18th- and 19th-century elections had similar rules to work out the winner.

Voters voted for one candidate in their area, known as a **SEAT** or **ELECTORAL DISTRICT**. The votes were quickly counted up and whoever got the most was elected. This is known as **PLURALITY** or the "first-past-the-post" system, possibly because politicians of the past liked horse-racing.

WOOHOO!

LOOK, I WON A SEAT.

It's still used today in the USA, India, and the UK, but boy, does it have its problems. For starters, a party might receive millions of votes across the country yet not win a single seat. All those voters now have no representation. That's tough!

Neither does it allow smaller parties much chance to win their fair share of seats. At the 2015 UK General Election, the Green Party won 1.1 million votes nationwide but only one out of the 650 seats. The Conservative Party polled 10 times as many votes but gained 330 times the number of seats. **NOT FAIR!**

At the same election, Alasdair McDonnell set a new UK record. Less than a quarter of all voters in his constituency voted for him, but he still won! When there are three, four, or more parties, the winner often receives less than half the total vote. This means more people voted AGAINST than FOR the winner. Doesn't sound very democratic, does it?

ELECTORAL UPGRADES

MAJORITY VOTING is a small upgrade on first-past-the-post. It's used to elect presidents in France, Brazil, and over 40 other countries. To win, a candidate needs more than **HALF THE VOTES**. Easy when there's only two in the contest, but when there's more, the candidates with the lowest votes drop out and another vote is held to find the winner.

A quite different electoral system tries to match the total votes each party receives with how many representatives they get. So, if the Breakfast Party won 33.33% of all the votes, they receive a third of all the seats.

We call this **PROPORTIONAL REPRESENTATION** or **PR** for short.

One of the first PR systems was drawn up by English schoolteacher Thomas Hill in 1819. He used it to elect school committees. Hill's son, Rowland, was involved in running Australia and insisted PR was used in the city of Adelaide's first council elections in 1840. A few months earlier, Hill's **PENNY BLACK** became the world's first proper postage stamp. Big year!

Before the end of the century, Denmark, Argentina, and Belgium were all using PR. It's now part of national elections in over 90 countries. Many claim it's fairer, plus smaller parties get representation. And with every vote counting, it encourages people to come out and vote.

PR costs more to operate and is more complicated. It also tends to produce no outright winner. When no party has more than half the seats, several parties may have to put aside their differences and work together to form a **COALITION GOVERNMENT**.

65

DEEDS NOT WORDS

Of course, choosing the perfect voting system is irrelevant for people who aren't even allowed to vote. Just 150 years ago, next to no women* around the world had **SUFFRAGE**: the right to vote in elections.

In 1893, **NEW ZEALAND** became the first country to welcome female voters in national elections after a long campaign led by Kate Sheppard. But elsewhere, some thought women too emotional or gullible to take part in politics. One British MP, Rowland Hunt, was most worried about the big hats women wore at the time blocking his view in parliament!

EVEN QUEEN VICTORIA THOUGHT WOMEN'S SUFFRAGE WAS "MAD, WICKED FOLLY"

But the opposition in Britain never deterred activist **EMMELINE PANKHURST**. She formed a new women's group in 1903, which carried out more extreme protests. These included hunger strikes, disrupting meetings and attacking male politicians. The **SUFFRAGETTES**, as they were known, believed that real change came from **DEEDS, NOT WORDS**. They faced arrest, imprisonment, and attacks from angry men in public as well as brutal police tactics.

*Many Native American tribes, like the Haudenosaunee, allowed female chieftains to vote at their councils.

One suffragette, **LEONORA COHEN**, smashed a glass case containing crown jewels in the Tower of London. She later disguised herself as a bread delivery man to help another suffragette escape capture.

One famous suffragette is **EMILY DAVISON**. She protested by running onto the course at the 1913 Epsom Derby horse race, losing her life in the fight for equality.

A team of female bodyguards, all trained in the martial art of Jiu-Jitsu, protected the suffragettes. Some carried clubs hidden under their dresses.

Their efforts encouraged women in other countries, too. Suffragette **ALICE PAUL** returned home to campaign in the US, helping to form the National Women's Party and amend the US Constitution to allow women to vote.

HOW TO STEAL AN ELECTION

As well as ensuring people's right to vote, it's important in a democracy that every vote is counted. But this is not always the case. Ballot boxes have been ~~stolen~~ (117 boxes in Nigeria, in 2011) or ~~destroyed~~. Elsewhere, boxes full of fake votes for one party have appeared and been counted as real votes.

ARE BALLOT BOXES ALWAYS THIS WARM?

INCINERATOR
BALLOT BOX

Despite laws against **ELECTORAL FRAUD,** voting officials sometimes struggle to keep an election clean and fair, especially when it's the people in power doing all the cheating.

One of the sneakiest tricks of all occurred in areas of **UKRAINE** known to oppose President Yanukovych. Voters there were handed brand-new pens to make their vote in 2004. A free pen—nice! But... they were filled with disappearing ink, so minutes after the vote was in the box, it turned blank and didn't count. **OUTRAGEOUS!**

I CAN'T BELIEVE THEY DIDN'T WANT TO SEE MY "VANISHING VOTES" TRICK.

BALLOT STUFFING is when extra, illegal votes are added during an election. Some occur due to the same person voting more than once. In the past, people have switched hats to confuse officials and in modern times, used false names including Mickey Mouse, Harry Potter, and Ham Sandwich!

ARE YOU SURE YOU ARE 71-YEAR-OLD GRANDMOTHER OF FOUR, MILLICENT FAWCETT?

YUP.

VOTE HERE

These *dirty tricks* and others, such as intimidation and threats, can lead to some seriously *suspicious* results, like the 2017 election in Turkmenistan where the sitting president gained 97.7% of all votes. Fishier still was the 1927 election in **LIBERIA**. There, Thomas Faulkner scooped 9,000 votes—brilliant, as there were only 15,000 voters in Liberia at the time. However, the president, Charles D.B. King, obtained 234,000: over 15 times as many as was possible!

Elections have been rigged by parties on both the left and right—often by those with extreme views one way or the other.

COMMUNISM AND FASCISM

During the 1920s, **extreme** left and right political ideas took hold in some European countries. To the **far left** was **COMMUNISM**, based on the theories of Karl Marx (see pages 56–57). It was established in Russia by Vladimir Lenin after the tsar—the Russian monarch—was overthrown.

Russia was renamed the **USSR** (Soviet Union) in 1922 and two years later, Lenin died and Josef Stalin took over, ruling until 1952.

To the **far right** was **FASCISM**, named by Benito Mussolini. His supporters marched into Rome in 1922, demanding that Italy's king put them in power. In next to no time, fascists controlled all of **ITALY**.

Fascism opposed communism and its idea of everyone sharing wealth. Instead, fascists believed in putting the country ahead of its people who should live in a rigid system where everyone knew their place.

FASCISM sought to appeal to people's pride in their country, but quickly twisted into racism and hatred of other peoples, especially with Adolf Hitler's Nazi Party in Germany. Hitler believed in a German "master race" and planned to wipe out Jews and other peoples the Nazis considered inferior. Horrifying.

They'd hate to admit it, but in many ways, fascist and communist countries in the 1920s and 1930s were remarkably similar.

OUT! went different political parties, proper elections, democracy, and freedom of speech. **IN!** came a dictator in charge, a one-party state, no opposition, or criticism allowed and total government control of the economy and society.

Yet, despite similarities, the two extremes would fight each other during the Spanish Civil War (1936–39) and World War II (1939–45). WWII remains the biggest conflict in history, and had a **BIG** impact on politics.

THE SOMETIMES UNITED NATIONS

After WWII, a plan was needed to to stop all that vicious fighting. The idea was born when one world leader interrupted another's bath time…

US President Franklin D. Roosevelt had a brainwave and told UK Prime Minister Winston Churchill all about it in 1942 during Churchill's stay (and bath) in the White House. The United Nations (UN) was designed to help keep the peace after WWII by talking rather than fighting.

TO JAW-JAW IS BETTER THAN TO WAR-WAR.

An actual quote from Churchill about the UN.

The UN was founded by 51 nations shortly after war ended in 1945. When South Sudan joined in 2006, it became the UN's 193rd member. With its HQ in New York, the UN's aim is to provide a safe space for international politics.

A secretary-general leads the UN, the latest being António Guterres who had previously been prime minister of Portugal. Other famous secretary-generals include Kofi Annan from Ghana and Ban Ki-moon from Korea.

The UN General Assembly is where talks and agreements are held. Every nation attends, and—whatever their size—each has an equal vote.

EAST TIMOR'S IN THE HOUSE!

ALL THE SMALL NATIONS, SAY YO!

Things get a bit more elitist when it comes to the UN Security Council. This group of 15 nations (China, USA, Russia, France, and the UK always, plus 10 others selected by rotation) tries to prevent conflicts flaring up. They can send some of the force of over 95,000 UN peacekeepers to protect civilians, distribute aid, and provide security during elections.

There've been plenty of feisty moments in the General Assembly, including Soviet leader Nikita Khrushchev banging his shoe on the table, and a few dull ones, such as the eight-hour speech given by Indian politician V.K. Menon in 1957.

The European countries who were especially affected by the fallout from WWII developed even closer ways of working together to keep the peace.

THE GREAT ~~28~~ OOPS, 27

In the years after **WORLD WAR II**, Europe was shattered.

As countries rebuilt, many vowed to work with rather than fight their neighbors. As well as global organizations like the United Nations, new bodies were founded in Europe, such as the **EUROPEAN ECONOMIC COMMUNITY** (EEC) in 1957. More nations joined, and in 1993 a closer alliance, called the **EUROPEAN UNION** (EU), was formed. This has its own courts, parliament, councils, and civil servants. People from EU countries can move and live freely in any other member country.

Each EU nation holds elections once every five years. Together, they elect 705 MEPs (Members of the European Parliament), who sit in Brussels in Belgium, and Strasbourg in France. The Parliament forms laws followed by all the member nations. When there's a clash, European law trumps the laws of individual nations.

The **EUROPEAN PARLIAMENT** is the single biggest employer of language interpreters in the world. With 24 official languages in the EU, there's an awful lot of translating to do.

The EU has admirers, but also critics. In 2016, the "stay-or-go" UK held a referendum, nicknamed **BREXIT**. **REMAINERS** felt the EU promoted close links between countries, helped the economy and made good environmental laws. **LEAVERS** wanted to stop following EU laws and sending it money. They also wanted the UK, not the EU, to control immigration to the country. Leave won (51.9% to 48.1%) and the UK officially left in January 2020.

That still leaves 27 nations in the EU from Finland in the east to Ireland and Portugal in the west. Portugal joined in 1977, a year after it had finally granted all women the vote. About time!

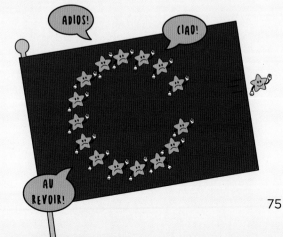

ABOUT TIME!

PORTUGAL was one of Europe's suffrage slow coaches. In **BULGARIA** in 1937, a woman could only vote in local elections if she was married and had children. And **LIECHTENSTEIN** was even worse, not giving women the vote until 1984!

FINLAND, in contrast, led the pack by granting women's right to vote and to stand as a candidate in elections in 1906. The following year, the world's first female MPs, 19 of 'em, were elected.

WORLD WAR I began in 1914 and saw a massive shortage of manpower in farms and factories—most men were off to battle. So, women stepped in to fill their boots… and did so, brilliantly. Many chauvinists who saw women as the "weaker sex" were stopped in their tracks.

YOU DO BELIEVE IN VOTES FOR WOMEN, DON'T YOU?

At the war's end in 1918, a whole host of nations gave some women the vote, such as, in the **UK**, 30+ year-olds who owned homes. This was altered to all women over 21 in 1928, the same year that **SWISS** women paraded a giant model snail to protest the oh-so-slow progress in a country where the men first voted in 1291, but women didn't get the vote in national elections until 1971!

The 1930s saw another stack of suffrage successes with **JAPAN, ITALY, CHINA,** and **INDIA** among others. Yet, by the time Sirimavo Bandaranaike became prime minister of **SRI LANKA** in 1960—the world's first elected female leader—women in some 50 other nations still couldn't vote. In **SAUDI ARABIA**, this was the case until 2015. Tut-tut!

In countries including Egypt, Pakistan, and India, it was the law of their colonial rulers (pages 58–59) that prevented women from voting. Soon after booting out the occupying empire, women were granted suffrage. Happy Independence Day!

INDEPENDENCE DAY

Just 12 years before the history-making election of Sirimavo Bandaranaike, Sri Lanka finally shook off the British Empire. And it wasn't alone: more than 50 nations gained **INDEPENDENCE** in the first 25 years after **WORLD WAR II**. There was another burst of independence in the 1990s. Half of the 30 new countries created then were the result of the break-up of the **SOVIET UNION**.

As independence celebrations wound down, these shiny new nations suddenly had to build a system of government. **BIG JOB!**

Some copied their former colonial rulers. The UK's system with a prime minister and parliament was mimicked by more than 20 new nations. Others opted to be led by a president, while some, like Mali, Belarus, and Fiji, had both a Prez and a prime minister.

Speaking of Fiji, their government was red-faced in 2010 when they lost their 1970 **DECLARATION OF INDEPENDENCE**. They had to ask Britain for a copy!

WELL, WHERE DID YOU SEE IT LAST?

Chad, Indonesia, and Ghana plumped for a **SINGLE ASSEMBLY** of lawmakers, while others went for two. Saint Lucia's second chamber contains just 11 elected members—no subs if they wanted to play soccer. In contrast, China's National People's Congress contains a whopping 2,987 members.

A handful of new nations, such as North Korea, Vietnam, and Eritrea, became **ONE-PARTY STATES** with no meaningful elections. Others started out as representative democracies with parliaments and elections, until the country's military decided to take the law into their own hands…

COUP YOU!

A **MILITARY COUP** (pronounced koo) is when some or all of a nation's armed forces overthrow their country's government. Some coups are violent with hundreds, even thousands, killed. Others are mostly peaceful with the army and other forces making a big show of force and the government wilting under the pressure.

Did you know there have been over 220 successful coups since the end of World War II? That's more coups than there are countries! **BOLIVIA** leads from the front with eight during that time.

The 1960s were coup-crazy, with a record 61 successful coups—and African colonel **CRISTOPHE SOGLO** was involved in three of them. He overthrew governments in Benin twice, made himself president, and then suffered a coup himself in 1967. More recent coups have changed governments in Thailand (2014), Zimbabwe (2017), Yemen and Sudan (both 2019).

A powerful, unhappy military and an unpopular, weak government are key coup ingredients. The armed forces may be concerned about their country and step in to help, or they might really want to grab permanent power for themselves.

Whatever the motivation, a successful coup takes plenty of organization.

Once a **COUP** secures power, there's often an uncertain period as the military tries to establish law and order. They may stay in power just long enough to oversee fair elections to form a new civilian government. Sometimes, though, the military stick around for years and countries may end up with a dictator in strict charge.

HOW TO COUP

- ☑ Occupy the assembly
- ☐ Arrest the president (try not to harm them… too much)
- ☐ Seize TV and radio stations
- ☐ Close airports
- ☐ Guard banks
- ☐ Seize control of power stations
- ☐ Address nation on TV
- ☐ Stop ministers fleeing

IRON GRIP

The 20th century saw many countries move from autocracy to democracy, but some nations chose a different path, caught in the iron grip of a strict, *authoritarian dictator.*

Authoritarian leaders aren't big at taking criticism on the chin. Their usual response is to throw a tantrum and imprison, torture, or kill their critics. On Christmas Eve, 1969, 150 opponents of Macias Nguema, dictator of **EQUATORIAL GUINEA**, were all shot by guards dressed up as Santa Claus.

Dictators often ban other political parties or make their life hard by harassing them and holding rigged elections impossible for opponents to win. TV news and newspapers are usually controlled, only broadcasting or printing what the dictator wants.

In **NORTH KOREA**, TVs and radios are sealed to prevent users tuning in to foreign broadcasts. The World Wide Web is banned in the country, as are blue jeans, Coca-Cola, and many hairstyles.

No one dares say no to an extreme dictator. It's far too risky. This often means that they can run riot with all sorts of crazy laws and schemes. Romanian dictator Nicolae Ceaușescu banned the board game Scrabble (too hard for him), while Haiti's dictator François Duvalier had all black dogs put down, fearing they were bad luck.

Dominican Republic dictator Rafael Trujillo started renaming things after himself including the country's capital city and its highest mountain. That's nothing compared to Turkmenistan president, Saparmurat Niyazov. During his rule (1990–2006), he created a national holiday for melons*, banned gold teeth, and made his book of poems and sayings a required part of the country's driving test!

*Second Sunday in August, in case you're interested.

RESTRICTED BY RACE

Speaking of tests, did you know that until 1965, voters had to pass reading and writing **TESTS** in some US states before they could vote? White people often received easy questions and even easier marking.

Questions for Black people, though, were often confusing and the marking really harsh. Can you answer this question below? Some tests had 30 questions like this to be answered in just 10 minutes.

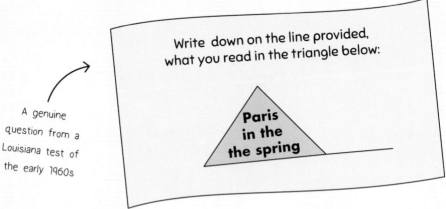

A genuine question from a Louisiana test of the early 1960s

Write down on the line provided, what you read in the triangle below:

Paris in the the spring

There was **NO RIGHT ANSWER**! Whatever you answered ("down," "Paris in the spring" or "what you read in the triangle below:") could be marked as wrong. Just one mistake equaled a failed test and no vote.

Other places in the US used a "GRANDFATHER CLAUSE" in voting laws where you could only vote if your grandad had—impossible for Black people whose ancestors had been enslaved, with no right to vote.

These *cruel tactics* were used to stop Black people from voting even though the US Constitution had been amended in 1870 to allow them to do so.

VOTING was just one of many aspects of life where, between the abolition of slavery in 1865 and the mid-1960s, Black people in America were treated like second-class citizens. In many US states, they were unable to choose where they lived, worked, ate, or went to school. This SEGREGATION even saw separate water fountains and bus seats for Black and white people.

A large CIVIL RIGHTS MOVEMENT rose up in the 1950s and led to huge marches and peaceful protests. Some of the most famous include the Montgomery Bus Boycott started by Rosa Parks, a Black woman who refused to give up her bus seat for a white passenger. People all over Montgomery, Alabama, began walking instead of using the bus, and eventually segregation on public transport was outlawed. Other successes included the 1965 Voting Rights Act, which banned literacy tests and some other barriers to voting, a move which also helped Native Americans.

BUT WE WERE HERE FIRST

It wasn't just Black Americans who had a l o n g wait for **SUFFRAGE**. Native Americans were only given the chance to become citizens and vote in 1924. **OUTRAGEOUS!**

It then took a further 40 years and lots of campaigning for all 50 states to actually grant the vote. Challenges to Native Americans voting in local and state elections still occur to this day.

> THEY MAKE US CITIZENS? PAH! WE'VE LIVED IN THESE LANDS FOR OVER 15,000 YEARS.

> COMPARED TO US, THEY'RE NEWBIES!

North of the border, the First Nations peoples of Canada had a similar struggle. First Nations peoples had a senator in the Canadian Parliament, **JAMES GLADSTONE** (1958), two years before they could actually vote in national elections.

> I WON— AND I DIDN'T EVEN GET MY OWN VOTE!

In Australia, Aboriginals and Torres Strait Islanders only gained the vote in 1962, but even then didn't have quite the same deal as other Australians. Enrolling to vote was only made compulsory for these native peoples in 1984.

In South Africa, a nationwide system of separating people by race began in 1948. This apartheid system forced different races to live and work apart, with Black people removed from their own land. White people ran the country despite being vastly outnumbered by Black people, who were given few rights.

Around the world, ordinary people protested against apartheid by refusing to buy South African goods, such as fruit and vegetables.

Despite this worldwide criticism, apartheid existed until 1990, causing terrible hardship. In 1993, a new constitution finally gave Black people the vote. Triumphant scenes greeted Nelson Mandela's election as South Africa's first Black president the following year.

YOU'RE KIDDING!

In South Africa, as in the vast majority of countries around the world today, turning 18 gives you the right to vote. In the past, you had to be older, up to a crummy 30 for the first women in the UK to get the vote in 1918!

Lowering the minimum age is called youth suffrage and it has resulted in dozens of countries dropping voting ages from 21 (like the US in 1971) or 19 (like South Korea in 2019) to 18.

There are arguments for and against lowering the **VOTING AGE** further to 16...

YES!

Teenagers can work full time, pay tax and be convicted of crimes at 16. In some countries, they can even serve in the armed forces. So, why should they not be able to vote? Young people are passionate about many political issues, such as climate change. Granting them the vote may connect them more with politics.

NO!

Some people think that younger teens may not know enough about the world to make a decision. They may be swayed by teen idols and influencers. They may simply not be mature enough to vote.

A handful of places have already gone sweet 16, such as **BRAZIL** in its 1988 constitution, **ARGENTINA** in 2012, and the **SCOTTISH PARLIAMENT** in 2015.

In 2007, **AUSTRIA** became the first European nation to make 16 the voting age for all elections. **CROATIA** and **TURKEY** have lowered the age of candidacy (the age you can compete in an election) to 18 for all their elections. That means a teenager could, in theory, try to become president. Imagine if they won!

Being able to vote is nice—now let's find out what that actually means.

GOING TO THE POLLS

BANG! The election is **ON** and **OFF** go the candidates. Every country runs their elections slightly differently, but all must collect, count, and declare votes.

Before election day, political parties, their staff, and candidates **CAMPAIGN** furiously. They use advertising, speeches, TV debates, and visits to the public to urge voters to vote for them. Much of their effort may be negative campaigning—explaining the faults of their opponents rather than their own merits.

I WON'T INDULGE IN NEGATIVE CAMPAIGNING, UNLIKE MY OPPONENT WHO DOESN'T PAY HIS TAXES, DOESN'T CARE ABOUT YOUR ISSUES AND HAS SMELLY FEET.

Most parties produce an **ELECTION MANIFESTO**—a collection of campaign promises they say they will keep if they get elected into power.

Some people cast their vote in advance or by mail, but most head to a local polling station on election day. There, they mark a **BALLOT PAPER** with the candidates' names printed on it or use a voting machine. In South Korea, voters stamp their ballot paper with red ink. The papers are either counted by hand or scanned by a counting machine.

In **GAMBIA**, since the 1960s, voters place marbles in drums each decorated with the candidate's photo and their party's colors and symbols. A bell sounds when the marble drops.

To avoid confusion, bicycles are banned near polling stations. Seriously.

RING
RING
RING

SORRY, SIR—I NEED YOU TO STOP TAMPERING WITH THE BALLOTS.

In elections contested by three or more parties, some people vote **TACTICALLY**. This means not voting for your first choice if you believe they are unlikely to win. Instead, you vote for a party or candidate who can stop your least-liked party from winning.

In 1803, Philip Dundas was elected MP for Gatton, England, by one vote to zero!

Elections usually involve a lot more counting than that. Some electoral districts see more than 100,000 votes cast in an election. All have to be added up and checked before the vote can be announced, even the votes of funny fringe candidates.

I DEMAND A RECOUNT!

SURPRISING CANDIDATES

Politics is a deadly serious business… usually. Some candidates don't get the memo, such as **MR. FISHFINGER** and **LORD BUCKETHEAD** who stood in the UK's 2017 General Election.

Many funny fringe candidates do it as a stunt or to highlight a single political issue. Sometimes, the votes they attract are a protest against the government or quality of the other candidates. This was the case in 1967 when a **BOTTLE OF FOOT POWDER** was elected **MAYOR** of Picoazá in Ecuador.

Eight years earlier, a female rhinoceros called Cacareco received 100,000 votes in council elections in Brazil. A protest vote in Brazil is now called a **"CACARECO VOTE."**

PROTEST PARTIES provide voters in some countries with a way of showing their distrust and unhappiness with politics. In 2014, the Shiji Seitō Nashi (No Party to Support) party won 104,854 votes in **JAPAN**.

Some jokes or protests though, turn more serious. In 1991, the Polish Beer Lovers Party won 16 seats in **POLAND**'s national parliament. In 2010, **ICELAND**'s Best Party promised free towels at swimming pools, a polar bear for the zoo, and not to carry out any of its election promises.

It ended up getting more votes than any other party in council elections and helped run Iceland's capital city, Reykjavik!

Even more extraordinary was **UKRAINE** comic Volodymyr Zelenskiy, who played the president in a TV sitcom in his country. In 2019, he stood to be the real-life president of Ukraine… and won with over 70% of the vote. It's not the only case of the media influencing politics.

GOOD NEWS AND BAD NEWS

TV and social media helped make a comedian a president. Along with newspapers, radio, billboards, and posters, they're the **MASS MEDIA** most used to communicate crucial news and political info to people—from the latest stats to the election promises of candidates.

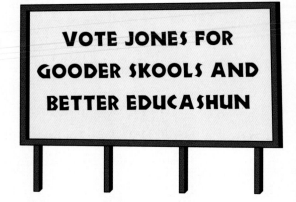

VOTE JONES FOR GOODER SKOOLS AND BETTER EDUCASHUN

NEWS MEDIA can act as a **WATCHDOG**. It can reveal false facts and claims, question and challenge politicians, and show how trustworthy they are and if they're capable of performing under pressure.

Journalists sometimes uncover lies and scandals so big, they bring down governments. This was the case in the 1970s when reporters discovered that President Richard Nixon covered up break-ins and thefts of information from his political rivals—the Watergate scandal. But it's not all good news...

The people who control the media can influence politics and voters' views by what news stories and politicians they choose to cover, and how. But the people who control the media are not elected. If you are rich enough, you can buy a newspaper or TV channel. That's not very democratic!

And there's more. Not all news is presented in a fair, balanced, way. When it isn't, it's said to be biased. Some news media is biased to reflect the viewpoint of its owner, or a particular political party.

BIASED MEDIA claims to tell you all the news, but it doesn't. It may omit crucial stories or interviewees that challenge its viewpoint. It may also only tell one side of a news story—the side that supports its beliefs or makes its opponents look wrong or foolish.

Biased media can also distort a story by blowing up one tiny aspect and making it appear more extreme than it is.

PUTTING PRESSURE ON

Who else, besides the media, force governments to respond to issues in between elections? Some groups try to change laws or government actions, but don't want to be in power themselves. These are known as **INTEREST** or **PRESSURE GROUPS**.

Pressure groups may focus on a single issue, such as the National Rifle Association (NRA), which protects Americans' right to own guns. Others campaign about a broad subject such as the environment (Greenpeace) or human rights (Amnesty International).

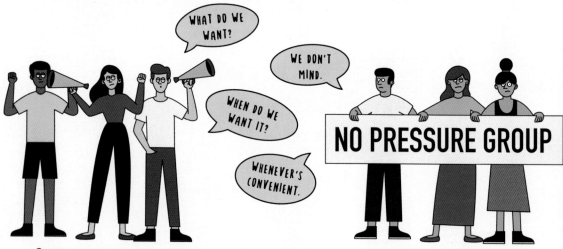

Some groups promote a particular industry, such as car-makers. Others represent a certain slice of society, such as single moms or military veterans. Pressure groups may create research on their subject and organize campaigns and publicity stunts to win public support.

They may challenge laws in courts or hire people called **LOBBYISTS** to try to persuade elected politicians to support their aims. To persuade them further, pressure groups in many countries help fund politicians' election campaigns or pledge that the group's members will vote for them.

Critics argue that when they lobby and fund politicians, pressure groups bypass elections and democracy. They carry out some of this work in secret, which may lead to bribes and corruption.

TO SUGGEST THAT I'M BEING FUNDED BY THE FIZZY DRINKS LOBBY IS *BURP* RIDICULOUS.

Larger, richer pressure groups may gain much more access to politicians than smaller groups. So, wealthy pressure groups representing big business, for example, might have more influence than a small environmental group who may struggle to be heard.

Those without a voice or easy access to politicians sometimes protest in other ways.

MAKING CHANGE HAPPEN

What else can people do between elections to get **CHANGE**?

Well, many join established pressure groups and campaign hard for change from there. Others write to their local elected politician or organize **PETITIONS**, collecting thousands, occasionally millions, of signatures.

A handful of petitions result in government action. In 2012, a law was about to be made in Illinois to stop cities from banning plastic bags. Abby Goldberg, just 13, organized a petition with 174,000 signatures sent to the state governor, which saw the law stopped.

Many change-makers use social media, websites, or pamphlets, and peaceful mass demonstrations (like US civil rights marches on page 85). They hope to change public opinion and attract media and politicians' attention.

Others, though, opt for more **EXTREME** techniques, such as occupying buildings or disrupting businesses and transport. Extinction Rebellion, for instance, have blocked roads and glued or chained themselves to trains in major cities including New York and London in protest against climate change.

REPEATED MASS PROTESTS can even see governments toppled. In 2011, pro-democracy protests began in Tunisia against their president of 23 years, Zine al-Abidine Ben Ali. They resulted in him fleeing the country with free elections held there later that year.

The mood of protest, known as the Arab Spring, spread to other nations nearby and saw autocratic leaders (remember them from page 82?) thrown out in Egypt, Libya, and Yemen. It has also sadly led to chaos and civil wars in the region. Not all protests are successful or end well.

NET GAINS

News of the **ARAB SPRING** was spread partly by messages and videos shared on social media. Many politicians are still catching up with how **SOCIAL MEDIA** can be used successfully. Sadly, it has already been hijacked at times by parties and interest groups to spread fake news—deliberate lies and exaggerations pretending to be true.

Fake news? Check by reading and watching lots of different sources.

PRESIDENT REALLY LIZARD ALIEN IN DISGUISE!

PRESIDENT: 'I'M DEFINITELY NOT A LIZARD ALIEN'

NEWS

What was definitely real news in 1997 was that astronaut **DAVID WOLF**, who was on the Mir space station, became the first to vote from space. He had to give his address as "low-Earth orbit" on his ballot paper, which he emailed back to the planet.

VOTE LIZARD ALIEN!

If internet voting can be done from space, why not on Earth? Wouldn't it boost turnout and be more convenient than traveling to a polling station? Estonians think so.

In 2005, Estonia introduced **I-VOTING** at nationwide elections. Voters use an ID card and card reader to register their vote over the internet. In Estonia's 2019 general election, 44% of voters used i-voting. A handful of other nations, like example Norway, have tried similar systems.

Why so few?

Well, many fear that **INTERNET SECURITY** isn't strong enough and who people voted for could be revealed, turning secret ballots into open ones. Worse, elections could be rigged or voting computers hacked and votes changed.

THE HACKER PARTY WIN WITH A STRANGELY HIGH 99% OF THE VOTE.

As politicians and governments all stayed at home during the 2020 coronavirus pandemic, politics began working virtually. Video calls and the internet replaced face-to-face meetings, while the European Parliament allowed its members to vote by email. Perhaps this will result in internet voting becoming more common in future, despite the added cost…

NO SUCCESS WITHOUT EXCESS?

Getting elected to school council may cost as little as photocopying some posters and flyers. But moving up through the political ranks, CAMPAIGN COSTS can soar.

The 2020 US PRESIDENTIAL ELECTION cost candidates Joe Biden and Donald Trump around $6.6 billion. Ouch! In total, US election campaigns in 2020 cost almost $14 billion—double the 2016 figure. Double ouch!

Where does all that money go? On staff, holding events, travel, and a **LOT** of advertising. And where does the money come from? From candidates' personal fortunes, but mostly DONATIONS from individuals, organizations, pressure groups, or businesses.

The **HUGE** sums involved cause big problems for the democratic system. Politicians can spend more time fundraising than governing, and the **MEGA** money needed for campaigns stop some worthy candidates from taking part.

The reliance on big **CAMPAIGN DONORS** also gives those rich individuals unfair influence on politicians.

To try and address these problems, like strict parents, some countries slap on a tight **SPENDING LIMIT**. In France, each presidential wannabe can splash out a max of around €21.5 million. In UK elections for MPs, parties can spend up to £30,000 per seat they try to win.

THIS CHOCOLATE CENTERPIECE IS A GREAT ADDITION TO MY CAMPAIGN LAUNCH PARTY. NOW WHERE ARE THE LEAFLETS?

ERR, THERE WASN'T ANY MONEY LEFT IN THE BUDGET FOR THEM...

WOOHOO, WE WON! NOW FOR A QUICK BIT OF GOVERNING, THEN IT'S BACK ON THE CAMPAIGN TRAIL...

VOTE

COSTS are also kept down by limiting how long a campaign can last—a max of 60 days in Argentina, but just 12 days in Japan. In contrast, campaigns to become US president can last 18 months—nearly half as long as the presidential term itself! These long campaigns mean costs really mount up.

Candidates and parties are not the only ones spending big. Holding elections can cost a fortune, especially in the world's biggest democracy.

POWER TO THE PEOPLE

The US presidential election may feel like the biggest game in town, but it's not the biggest democratic election. That's found in **INDIA**—home to over 910 million voters.

In 2019, a **GENERAL ELECTION** was held to pick the 543 members of the Lok Sabha—one of India's houses of parliament. A growing population meant there were 84.3 million more voters than the previous time (2014)—this is like adding all of Germany at a stroke! The election was a monster operation, lasting 39 days and costing over $7 billion.

Under Indian law, no person should have to travel more than 2 km to vote. In a country so vast, this meant setting up a staggering 1,035,918 polling stations. 11 million officials, police, and soldiers (that's more than everyone in Sweden) were involved. Many had to travel up Himalayan mountains, into tiger-filled forests, and through crocodile-infested swamps.

I LOVE A SNAP! ELECTION.

Trucks, helicopters, boats, and even elephants were used to reach voters. One polling station was set up deep inside the dense Gir forest... for just one voter: Mahant Bharatdas Bapu, a temple priest. That's democratic dedication for you!

WE REALLY NEED THAT INTERNET VOTING SYSTEM, LIKE THE ESTONIANS!

After voting, people receive a mark of semi-permanent **PURPLE INK** on the nail and cuticle of their index finger as an indication that they have cast their vote, so they cannot try to vote again.

In the end, over 613 million people voted, a turnout* of 67%. Not bad, but couldn't it be higher? How could more people be encouraged to take part and use their democratic right?

OOH, ELECTION PURPLE, MY FAVORITE SHADE...

*Turnout means the percentage of people who could vote who actually do vote.

TACKLING TURNOUT

The **RIGHT TO VOTE** in elections was hard-fought for in many countries. Despite this, many people who can vote today don't. Some may have fair reasons—from difficulties in getting to a polling station to being fearful of bullying or threats when voting. But many people who don't vote really don't have that much stopping them apart from their attitude.

For **NATIONAL ELECTIONS**, it's pats on the back all around if two-thirds of voters actually turn up. South Korea's 2017 elections saw 77% of voters make the effort. Well done! But many elections see lower turnouts. Less than 56% of all voting-age Americans voted in the 2016 presidential election, while less than half of eligible voters (48%) voted in Japan's 2018 elections.

TURNOUT drops even lower for most **LOCAL ELECTIONS**. Just 6.1% voted in 2015 to choose the mayor of Dallas, Texas.

One solution is to make voting **COMPULSORY** by law. This is the case in some 20 countries, including Belgium (the first, in 1894), Australia, and Singapore. In all three, voter turnout tends to be 90% or higher.

In these countries, not voting means you usually face a fine (€10–€25 in Belgium). In Greece, up until 2000, not voting meant you couldn't get a new driving license. Even tougher are current rules in Bolivia. Failure to vote means you may struggle to get your money out of a bank!

Other solutions to low turnout are to make registering to vote and voting a lot easier and to find ways of involving people in politics more, especially young people.

NEVER TOO YOUNG

One problem with politics is many young people think it has little to do with them. They feel it's all **DESPERATELY OLD** adults in charge.

SIR, WILL YOU SIGN THE LEGISLATION BEFORE OR AFTER YOUR NAP?

They have a point. In 2020, the **US PRESIDENTIAL ELECTION** was between 74-year-old Donald Trump and 77-year-old Joe Biden, while Cuba's leader, Raul Castro, was 89. Earlier that year, Malaysia's prime minister, Mahathir bin Mohamad, finally quit at the age of 94!

But is that all changing? In recent years, **YOUNG FEMALE POLITICIANS** have become PMs of New Zealand (Jacinda Ardern, 37) and Finland (Sanna Marin, 34), while Sebastian Kurz (31) became Chancellor of Austria in 2017. France, Italy, and Ireland have each elected their youngest ever leaders (all in their 30s) as well.

Parliaments and assemblies boast some even fresher faces. In 2015, 20-year-old Mhairi Black became the youngest British MP since 1832! Three years earlier, **PROSCOVIA ALENGOT OROMAIT** finished high school and then, at 19, became Africa's youngest MP—in Uganda's parliament.

I HAVEN'T BEEN THIS HAPPY SINCE I PASSED MY SCHOOL EXAMS, A FEW MONTHS AGO!

The **AGE OF CANDIDACY** in most countries (mostly between 18 and 25) stops school and college kids getting elected. But it doesn't mean they cannot have an impact. Just think of one teenager... **GRETA THUNBERG**.

And what about Pakistani education campaigner **MALALA YOUSAFZAI**? She was only 17 when she won the 2014 Nobel Peace Prize.

It's not just Greta and Malala. Thousands of teens and tweens are getting politically active worldwide—from learning about issues to running for school council or organizing online petitions and campaigns. Some of these will be our politicians and leaders of the future.

WHAT HAPPENS NEXT?

No one has a crystal ball. Well, actually, quite a few people do, but none can peer into it and predict what the future will bring. It's fun to guess, though!

As the world is constantly changing, politics will, too, as people demand change or they face new challenges. One likely prediction is that **TECHNOLOGY** will creep more and more into politics and government.

Citizens in future states may take part in **DIRECT DEMOCRACY**, like in ancient Athens but with women allowed this time. They might meet virtually over the internet in e-assemblies and vote directly on individual issues and laws, just like elected representatives do now.

Voter fatigue might become an issue, so perhaps there will be rewards or incentives for taking part… or punishments for not doing so.

Some countries may split up into smaller states, while others may band together in political or economic **UNIONS**. Democracy may arrive in some places for the first time, but leave others as authoritarian leaders take control.

Another future threat to democracy may be **TRANSNATIONAL CORPORATIONS** (TNCs). These giant companies are already wealthier than many countries. In the future, they may wield even more power than national governments and all without people having a say in their decisions.

Perhaps, in the distant future, the idea of borders between nations may prove old news as everyone deals with planet-wide problems. Who knows? One day, all of Earth might be run by a single, global government—a **COSMOCRACY**.

POLITICS TIMELINE

~3100 BCE

King Narmer unites Egypt and serves as its first ruler. Later rulers are known as pharaohs and claim their authority to govern comes from Egyptian gods.

509 BCE

Rome removes its last king, Tarquinius Superbus, and becomes a republic. A year later, the Greek city-state of Athens engages in direct democracy, with all male citizens able to vote and speak in a city gathering called the Assembly.

1734

Swedish women who pay taxes and own property are allowed to vote in local elections in the countryside—among the first European women to gain the right.

1215

The Magna Carta (meaning Great Charter) is signed by England's King John. It's one of the first documents to try to limit the absolute power of a king and give his subjects key rights.

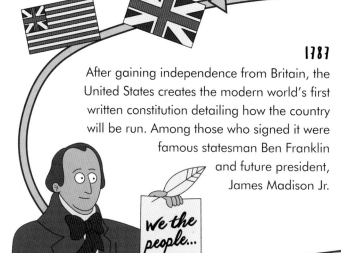

1787

After gaining independence from Britain, the United States creates the modern world's first written constitution detailing how the country will be run. Among those who signed it were famous statesman Ben Franklin and future president, James Madison Jr.

We the people...

1789

In a big year, George Washington is elected the first president of the United States and the French Revolution kicks off. It topples France's monarchy, which had ruled continuously for over 800 years.

221 BCE

The Qin dynasty in China begins, as the country is ruled by its first emperor, Qin Shi Huang. Over the centuries, a large bureaucracy of highly trained civil servants run the empire, a model copied by other states.

27 BCE

Rome goes from a republic to an empire, when it chooses to be ruled by an emperor. The Roman Empire lasts for 500 years until Rome is invaded by barbarians.

930 CE

The Althing in Iceland forms as an assembly or parliament for Viking settlers to agree on laws and sort out differences of opinion.

800s CE ONWARD

Parts of Europe are run under a feudal system where land is lent out in return for loyalty and wealth. Bottom of the pile are ordinary peasants known as serfs with few rights and tough lives.

1800

The White House, official home of the US president, is completed. It now features 123 rooms and an indoor swimming pool hidden under a press briefing room, but didn't have running water or an indoor toilet for its first 33 years.

1840s

A time of great unrest in Europe, with many failed revolutions and protests for more participation in politics. During this period, Karl Marx and Friedrich Engels write *The Communist Manifesto*, which will prove very influential.

1893

New Zealand grants all women the right to vote in parliamentary elections, but doesn't let them stand as candidates themselves until 1919. Boooo!

1917

The Russian Revolution results in the overthrow of the tsar as ruler and the establishment of the first large communist country—named the Soviet Union (USSR) in 1922. Until its break-up in 1991, it is the largest country in the world by area.

1994

Apartheid ends and the first elections involving all races in South Africa are held. Nelson Mandela becomes the first democratically elected president of the country.

1988

Teenagers rejoice! In its new constitution, Brazil lowers the minimum age you can vote in elections to 16. Nicaraguans wonder what all the fuss is about, as their country lowered the age four years earlier.

2005

Estonia introduces voting at elections using the internet. Click, Vote, Like. Nice.

2015

Saudi Arabia finally gives women the right to vote in elections. In the same year, North Korea claims that 99.97% of voters turned out in local elections, and all vote for the one party which controls the country.

1920s

The rise of extreme-right fascist parties in Italy and later Spain and the National-Socialist (Nazi) party in Germany. Their anti-democratic, anti-communist beliefs put them on a crash course with much of the rest of Europe, leading to World War II.

FAR RIGHT: FASCISM

FAR LEFT: COMMUNISM

1945

World War II ends with victory for the Allied powers and the establishment of the United Nations (UN) to act as a place where nations can settle their differences peacefully.

1960

A BIG year for African independence with 17, yes 17, new nations officially free of colonial powers, including Nigeria, Chad, and Togo. Flag-makers work overtime!

1949

The Chinese Communist Party completes a revolution to take control of the country, naming it the People's Republic of China.

ADIOS!

2016

The UK votes to leave the European Union, the first nation to do so, after a referendum attracts 33,577,342 votes.

2020

The Covid-19 pandemic sweeps the world. Most politicians stay at home and campaign or govern using emails and video calls. Joe Biden becomes the 46th President with 83.3 million votes, 7 million more than the sitting president, Donald Trump.

POLITICALLY PECULIAR

Politics has thrown up plenty of strange leaders, laws, and decisions. These include Russian ruler, Tsar Peter I who started **TAXING** beards in 1698 or the 1993 Italian law that allows local councils to tax businesses €100 if their shop signs cast shadows on pavements.

Banned objects according to **LAWS** include water pistols in Cambodia, chewing gum in Singapore, and building sandcastles on the beach in Eraclea, Italy.

While famed scientist Albert Einstein was asked to become president of Israel in 1952 but turned it down, many celebrities have moved into politics. These include actor-turned-**US** President Ronald Reagan; soccer star George Weah, who became president of **LIBERIA** in 2017; and cricket legend Imran Khan, who in 2018 was appointed prime minister of **PAKISTAN**.

Few are as humble as José Mujica, the president of **URUGUAY** from 2010 to 2015. He gave away 90% of his presidential pay to charity every month and lived simply in a tiny house instead of the presidential palace. He also drove a 25-year-old car rather than ride in a big limo.

Thankfully, only some politicians' behavior is as bizarre as General Ne Win, ruler of **MYANMAR** from 1962 to 1988. He shut off the country from the outside world, bathed in dolphin blood to stay young, and governed using fortune tellers and soothsayers. He changed the country's banknotes, for example, to numbers divisible by the number 9 and would shoot mirrors as a charm to protect himself against attack. Hey, who ever said politics was boring?

POLITICS QUIZ

Now you've read the entire quick history of politics, can you stand up to some tough questioning just like a politician in an interview?

1. In which Greek city-state did direct democracy begin?
a) Corinth   b) Sparta   c) Athens

2. What sort of animal was Cacareco, winner of a council election in Brazil?

3. Which Asian country was the first to have a female leader voted for in elections?

4. How many senators does the US Senate contain?

5. In which country did Mr. Fishfinger stand for election in 2017?

6. What name was given to the group led by Emmeline Pankhurst who campaigned for women's right to vote?

7. Which branch of government usually makes and debates laws?

8. In what year did Karl Marx and Friedrich Engels write *The Communist Manifesto*: 1776, 1848, or 1917?

9. Which small European country was the first in the world to allow internet voting at elections?

10. What word, beginning with the letter c, describes when two or more parties all work together to form a government?

11. Which country's parliament is called the Althing and heard a dispute involving Thord The Bellower?

12. In which city would you find the headquarters of the United Nations?

13. Can you name the country which only gave women the right to vote in 2015?

14. Which board game was banned as too difficult by Romanian dictator Nicolae Ceausescu?

15. Which country lost its independence document in 2010 and had to ask the UK for a copy?

16. In Germany's federal system of government, how many Länder, like Bavaria and Saxony, is the country divided into?

17. Which US governor (and, later, vice president) gave his name to the practice of reshaping voting districts to give your side an advantage?

18. What word means a state where religious beliefs guide all laws and decision-making?

Answers

1. c) Athens
2. A rhinoceros
3. Sri Lanka
4. 100
5. The UK
6. The Suffragettes
7. The legislative branch or legislature
8. 1848
9. Estonia
10. Coalition
11. Iceland
12. New York
13. Saudi Arabia
14. Scrabble
15. Fiji
16. 16
17. Elbridge Gerry (gerrymandering)
18. Theocracy

MORE POWER TO THE PEOPLE

Want to know more? Of course you do! Politics is a big, complex subject and every country (and sometimes region) runs its elections and governments in different ways. The more you learn from these books and websites, the more you can understand how politics works all over the world.

BOOKS

Girls Resist!: A Guide to Activism, Leadership, and Starting a Revolution— KaeLyn Rich (Quirk Books, 2018)
A handbook of ideas for young activists wanting to make a difference.

Vote for Me! Democracies, Dictators and Decision-makers—Louise Spilsbury (Wayland, 2017)
An entertaining look at different types of leadership and political systems around the world.

All about Politics (DK, 2016)
Magazine-styled visual guide to political issues and how governments work.

Politics for Beginners—Alex Frith, Rosie Hore, Louie Stowell (Usborne, 2017)
A good, all around look at different parts of politics and government from elections to ideologies and big political issues.

You Can Change the World—Margaret Rooke (Jessica Kingsley Publishers, 2019)
Interesting and inspiring stories about teens campaigning for change in politics and other walks of life.

Suffragettes and the Fight for the Vote—Sarah Ridley (Franklin Watts, 2019)
The story of women's fight for the right to vote, focusing on the UK.

FOR OLDER READERS

The Politics Book (DK, 2015)
A look at famous political thinkers throughout the ages and the ideologies and movements they helped form.

WEBSITES

https://www.everyvotecounts.org.uk/how-politics-works/
A series of guides to how parliamentary politics and elections work in the UK.

https://www.simplepolitics.co.uk/the-explainers/
Search by category for simple, infographic-based answers to questions about UK politics as well as more general political theory.

http://gws.ala.org/category/social-sciences/politics-government
A collection of links to handy websites about US politics.

http://www.democracy-building.info/systems-democracy.html
Text-only but very useful guide, comparing the different forms of democracy.

https://www.abc.net.au/btn/classroom/what-is-democracy/10524786
A short video from Australia about how democracy developed.

https://www.summer.harvard.edu/inside-summer/4-tips-spotting-fake-news-story
Sift out the fake news from the true news using these four handy tips and links from Harvard University.

https://www.youtube.com/watch?v=QoIafzc0k74
This brief video describes how the United Nations works.

GLOSSARY

ABSOLUTE MONARCHY A form of government where a king or queen holds all political power.

AUTHORITARIAN A system where the government has strict control over the country and its people, giving them few freedoms and frequently outlawing elections and freedom of speech.

AUTOCRACY Rule by a single person such as a king, queen, or emperor.

BIAS To not hold a neutral view but to lean in favor or against a particular thing such as a person, political idea, or policy.

CANDIDATE A person who competes to be elected for a political role.

CITIZEN A person who is a member of a country or state. Citizens have certain duties and rights.

CIVIL SERVANT A person who is not elected but works for the government.

CIVIL WAR A war between different groups of people from the same country.

COALITION When two or more parties govern together, when neither has an overall majority.

COLONY A country or region under the control of another country, often occupied by settlers from that country.

CONSTITUTION The system of rules and principles that describe how a country is run.

DEMOCRACY Government by the people, through direct votes (direct democracy) or elections to pick people to represent their views (representative democracy).

ELECTORATE All the people able to vote in an election.

EUROPEAN UNION (EU) A political, economic, and social union of 27 countries in Europe.

EXECUTIVE The branch of government in charge of running the country. It may come up with ideas for laws and ensures that laws and decisions are carried out.

FEDERALISM A system of government where power is shared between two or more levels such as a central, nationwide government and local, state, or regional governments.

HUMAN RIGHTS Basic, fundamental rights that all people should have including the rights to life, food, and not to be harmed by others.

JUDICIARY The branch of a country's government responsible for judging and ruling on laws.

LEGISLATURE The branch of government that has the power to make and change laws.

MANIFESTO A written set of aims and policies should they get into government that a political party publishes before an election.

POLLING STATION Name given to a building or location where votes are cast during an election.

PR Short for proportional representation—types of voting systems in which the share of seats a party wins matches the share of the vote it receives.

PRESSURE GROUP A group of people who work together to try to influence what other people or the government think about a particular issue.

REPRESENTATIVE DEMOCRACY A system of government where voters elect people to represent them in government and make decisions on their behalf.

SUFFRAGE The right to vote in political elections.

THEOCRACY A form of government which makes its laws based on religious beliefs and writings.

INDEX

ALSO AVAILABLE IN THE SERIES

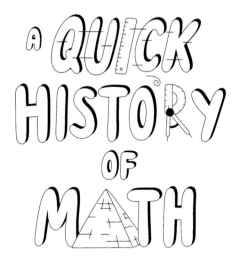

This rip-roaring rundown of the whole **HISTORY OF MATH** takes us from counting cavemen to today's big data wizards using math to solve crimes, checking out how math has changed and changed the world along the way.

From the beginning of **TIME** itself, to the formation of **STARS** and **PLANETS** and even the **EVOLUTION** of human beings, this joke-packed intergalactic history will get you up to speed on the last 13.8 billion years.

A QUICK HISTORY OF MONEY

The history of **BUYING, SELLING, SAVING**, and **STEALING** is full of crazy stories and unbelievable facts, proving that while it might sound all grown-up and serious, **MONEY** sure is funny.

CLIVE GIFFORD is an award-winning author of books for children and young adults. His fiction and non-fiction cover a huge breadth of topics, including refugees, the arms trade, and famous world leaders from throughout history. Clive holds a BSc in Political Science. A contributor to Encyclopedia Britannica, his books have won awards from the Royal Society, Blue Peter, PBS, Smithsonian, and School Library Association. Clive lives in Manchester, UK.

Brimming with creative inspiration, how-to projects, and useful information to enrich your everyday life, Quarto Knows is a favorite destination for those pursuing their interests and passions. Visit our site and dig deeper with our books into your area of interest: Quarto Creates, Quarto Cooks, Quarto Homes, Quarto Lives, Quarto Drives, Quarto Explores, Quarto Gifts, or Quarto Kids.

A Quick History of Politics © 2021 Quarto Publishing plc.
Text © 2021 Clive Gifford
Illustrations © 2021 Steve Gavan

First published in 2021 by Wide Eyed Editions, an imprint of The Quarto Group.
100 Cummings Center, Suite 265D, Beverly, MA 01915, USA.
T +1 978-282-9590 **www.QuartoKnows.com**

A CIP record for this book is available from the Library of Congress.
ISBN 978-0-7112-6274-4
eISBN 978-0-7112-6313-0

The illustrations were created artwork created with digital media
Set in Futura

Published by Georgia Amson-Bradshaw
Designed by Myrto Dimitrakoulia
Edited by Alex Hithersay
Production by Dawn Cameron

Manufactured in Singapore

1 3 5 7 9 8 6 4 2